Weird on Top

POEMS FOR THE DAVID LYNCH FILM

Wild at Heart

BECAUSE I AM EVERY CHARACTER IN THAT BOOK

* NETTIE ZAN *

Hagstone Books is the sole publisher of Nettie Zan
nee Jeanette Powers, JStar, Sparkle Princess, JBalls, et al and etc.
That's me.
I do not believe in intellectual property rights, so take
take take and use as you wish in any imaginable way.
Let me know if you want, it's so fucking rad
when we work and share together.

ISBN: 979-8-88596-979-6

Hagstone Books
KCMO 2022
nettiezan@gmail.com

every love story begins
with a match
this is how we learn
to hold our breath
consumed by fire

the fire will live on
in the child's head
she will watch her father
eat the kerosene
and her song is a red
candle in bed a lit cigarette
a burning automobile

this is how we summon
love and evil and death
I fell for you, baby
like a bomb
daddy's advice
amounts to
destroy me, peanut

every great love story begins
with a dead father
and a girl
a strike
looking for a match

Wrong. It's always better to blow a hole through the back of the head, right through to the bridge of the nose. Lots of irreparable brain damage.

--Marietta Fortune

you can't find love in hell
when you are the devil
and you're not a mother
unless you want to destroy
your daughter and her youth

pink nails and green olives
dirty girl dirty martini
bleeding lipstick
across your wrists
bared teeth
and assassination attempts
are nothing next
to her wide eyed
insult when the hostage
tries to escape
baby face covered in blood

bye bye daddy
bye bye boyfriends
you never did know
how to keep a man

a good girl keeps a photo
of Mother on the coffee table
where ice won't put out a fire

a good mother loves a man
who is always in a killin mood
her toes pointing to the ceiling
while a dog barks at
the prayer between her legs

sex is always tomorrow
and the scale is forever tattle
telling about what dies
when an old lady
wants her face back

when you are born into an inferno
the only thing that feels like home
is another pack of Marlboros
while you are jumping parole
to save the life of the woman
who stands by you
the way no one else ever has

fan blades on naked bodies
wrapped in white sheets
gray ash staining teeth
and black hearts singed
with bad ideas dancing
to Elvis metal croons

all I ask is please, please love me
oh yeah

how can anyone know right
from plain wrong a dog runs off
with a stolen severed hand
and there's no one to stop him
it's hungry on the road
and sometimes you gotta go
because love to the death
means you are the killing floor

breathing smoke
a mermaid in a plastic case
blonde curls falling for you
wearing a candy necklace
40 flavors of 4 years old
seems only to lead to another
set of bars in New Orleans
another cage in the penitentiary

you are the roadside collision
and watching yourself die
every time she puts her lipstick on
she'd go to the end of the world for you
but you know you are headed
straight back to the inferno
you don't know what it means
to not be on the run

live by your own code, Sailor
the stars don't lead anywhere you know
one day you'll be walking smoking shouting
and still half dead lying in the street
when a thug asks if you've had enough

you're gonna have to say yes

This is a snakeskin jacket!
And for me it's a symbol of my individuality,
and my belief in personal freedom.

--Sailor Ripley

when the whole rest of the world
got you under the house
and cut out your tongue
there's nothing left
but to go on the run
with the only Sailor you love

dancing on a motel bed
in a coral dress with a choker necklace
and a man who doesn't flinch
when you light a cigarette
and blow smoke through hoop earrings
into the aftermath of just another collision

he knows it aint exactly Emerald City
and you know there aren't enough Kools
to put out the cataclysm that began
with a bloody mouth curled up
on a bed in your Mother's house
a curette in your uncle's hand
and didn't end at the first baby
you killed with curlers in your hair

there's another headless pin-up girl
postered on the wall and peeling away
painting your nails red in bed
and the smell of puke never leaves

you know it means only one thing

bee bop a Lula, she's my baby

life's a jinx and you don't mean maybe
you're gonna keep on loving him
the crystal ball foretells
the feed store robbery
and you are still hungry
22 months and 18 days later
5 years, 10 months and 21 days later
9 months 13 days later

your crying will get so ugly
it becomes your mother's laugh

you'll click your heels three times
and find yourself on a city street
in bumper-to-bumper traffic
climbing over the windows
into your true love's arms
and not everyone gets that

but the two of you will spin
on the roof of your topless car
until the credits roll

shadow people understand
why cockroaches hide from the light
it's about being a peripheral being
where run and hide is part
of how you survive

even though
over the rainbow
and stockings stuffed
with figs and candy canes
and gifts under a shining tree
are all a person locked in the dark
really wants

to be someone that folks
leave cookies and milk for
instead of being dropped
at home by a police cruiser again
instead of mother searching you out
in fear with a flashlight poking around
while you are just making your lunch

what if the children smiled
and gave you lists of what joy is
what if you were the star
of the season and it was never July again

the summer heat needs rain
the rain makes filth and mud
and that's why you need black rubber gloves
you know you can never be clean
when people think you are filthy
it's just another bad idea
in a burning world of being
everyone's bowling pin
and as much as you want it
Christmas can't last all year

so you come to kiss a cockroach
in the darkest place of the body
you love what is unlovable edge
you are hem, perimeter and fringe
something borderline
that no one wants in the house

one day you will realize that the alien
wearing black gloves is you and you alone

and then you will lose your shiny Santa boots
mother will stop spying on you from the next room
you will learn a hard plastic lesson
all the shadows will have no light
and you will never be seen again

Aunt Rootie told Dell that one day he would realize that the alien wearing the black gloves was him, and him alone.

-- Lula Pace Fortune

You are one big, stupid asshole.

--Perdita Durango

Silver Coin: Perdita Durango

every mother knows
the only way to survive hell
is to pay the devil in pain
so you name your daughter
after lasting loss and then at least one person
has burned the truth into her body
she must receive the deep tap root
that is a woman's due torture:
look pretty and swallow hard

wear a black leather dress
to breakfast, red snakeskin high heels
to fry potatoes and wait for him
sit alone on your blood leather couch
only buy one lawn chair
because it's just you and the dust
and learn quick that bleach
doesn't get you clean
but men do love blonde hair
and you know you'll hand over
any silver coin that comes your way
in hopes that this one stays

he's a Black Angel
like your long-gone daddy
he knows murder is high love
that all women smell of flies

eating vomit on an unwashed rug
you are his grinning voodoo doll, a prop
for his ill intentions and greed
and you smile, say nothing
let the dagger earring swing
with your hips like mother did
set fire to anyone with a wife
turn in a friend on a dime
just to imagine a small licking
signal flame of love of your very own

who murders for you?
the crucifix on the wall
has never prayed for your sins
your charm is a jinx that left you cold in the desert
you only exist when you are useful
for someone else's story
arrange the empty gun
call the cops from a payphone
antagonize the jack rabbit to sheer fury
nobody ever looked for the bag of feed store money
with the devil's head blown off by his very own shotgun
and a poor lost boy angel crying
                              Lula!
and writhing in the dust

so light a match, lie to your friend
eat his evil eye like an olive
learn how to stage an accident

My Dog Barks Some: Bosey "Double Ought" Spool

a pornographer
is the rocket scientist
of what makes a man
go boom

you are picturing
in your mind
a beautiful blonde
with a head full of curls
and barking for cum

she's over the yellow
brick road and waiting
on the gold
and Toto's run away again

he's jerking off
to three dancing fat women
with real smiles on their painted faces
and you call this so Lynchian

we know
that my dog is always with me

it's your own mental picture
a white towel in a death grip
a hand on your shoulder

pushing you on
holding you back
double ought
is buckshot for large animal
hunting, like deer or …

just one man
lunging at you
a spark of incandescent fire
appears and disappears

this is love on the run
pale, wide-eyed
surrounded by cowboys
drinking tequila and Jack

he barks
they dance and shimmy

you are the dog
you are always with you

I don't mean your head-head.
I'm not gonna piss on your head, your hair and all,
I'm just gonna piss in the toilet. Y'all take a listen,
you'll hear the deep sound comin' down from
Bobby Peru.

When your body
needs to be held
so completely
it begins to not matter
if the hands are
the force of a gripping
insistence against you
or if the hands are
radio signals in the darkness
searching for life

it's not impossible to think
you want to be a Christmas present
a bunny rabbit racing nowhere
you start to want
to have your heart torn out
if only to feel just one something
to feel wanted

the body responds to bad teeth
his thumbs at your windpipe
the pressure on a nipple's gasp
you feel him breathing on you
and he keeps telling you
what you want
until you don't exist

you don't come up for air
and just want what he wants

it makes sense
to be a mirror
a flat reflection of the self
pantomiming
the kind of violent force
of fire, rage and death
that you are born into

and it's no surprise
when the villain lets go
and laughs at your sore jaw
your growing body
when you say *fuck me*
and he backs off
someday honey I will
but I gotta get going

and the only thing you can do right
is let him walk out that door
and never come back

life is all feed, fight or fuck
and it takes more than two men
to get the job done, but they'll never
admit they need an eager woman
in the driver's seat
to take the wheel and somehow get away
while the wreckage of their lives
are burning on the side of the road

you can only pass so many dead bodies
before the omens inspire a yawn
and violence is the only weapon you draw
a match ignites against the phosphorous
a fire is a bouquet made of teeth
yellow, rotten to the gums
the men grin and grimace
with their faces covered
in your last two pair
of sheer pantyhose

maybe he's doing it for you, baby
maybe he thinks this is the only way
he can raise a child in this wicked world
begin with a double ought sawed off, son
put on your snakeskin jacket, kid
it's a symbol of your personal freedom

they give it back when you get out
of the penitentiary and the clink
of glasses is toasting to the everlasting

maybe he's doing it because he doesn't know
any other way of doing things
does anyone know anyone
who was raised right?

it's all a set up, anyway
this whole world is wild at heart
and weird on top
so these two wolves take their shot
and can't help but create another accident
on the side of the road
no one notices anymore anyway
it's just another round in the shotgun
and five more years in a 4x10 room

when you are living proof
that bouquets are only meant
for lying on top of fresh dirt
and you only rest
when you are in that coffin

a blind man pouring gasoline
can see that there really has been
a build up of traffic these days

everybody got something to run away from
and only the lucky ever get something
to run to, and that's if they manage
to dodge the pile ups, lung cancer
being drowned with your sister and brother
by your mother, and ain't nobody who
doesn't get raped or robbed somewhere
on the road to wherever the rainbow is over

maybe you are one of the lucky ones
if you get your nose broken by thugs
in the street while you are running away
from your one shot at love

sometimes a good beating wakes you up
to the Good Witch in her pink fluff
with red stars and love for lifetimes
who calls you out on your shit
and sends you packing back
to the one big curl blonde
in polka dots with your son
and you wake up to the man
with a dagger on his shirt

and a boot on your nose
and learn what it means
to beg forgiveness
even if you don't know
what all you did wrong

you tell that glowing apparition
again about how you ain't worth nothing
but she won't listen
she sings you hope and glow up so
you'll fight for your dreams
don't turn away from love

and this makes enough sense to run
to face the traffic jam she's sitting in
the dashboard wrapped in zebra skin
to leap on top of a flaming car
and dance your way
back to the only place you belong

and here, on top of the get-a-way car
is where you sing that old Elvis song to your wife

love me tender, love me true

now you know what you are fighting for

Lula!

many special thanks to Jason Ryberg for showing me this film for the first time just a few years ago, and to Kim Vodicka for her incredible edits to the book. And of course to David Lynch for being in the Narrative Dada wheelhouse

Nettie Zan is an artist living in Kansas City and working on building community and creativity. You can buy their books at nettiezan.bigcartel.com and follow them on some social media probably.

What movie are you every character in?

also by Nettie Zan

Poems for Alcoholics
Ozark Love Poems
Dandylion Riot
Victimless Crime
America Stabbed James T Kirk
in the Arm with a #2 Pencil
Sparkle Princess vs Suicidal Phoenix
Little Jenny Sue
Don't Lose Your Head
Dead Things I Excrete
Perfectly Good Muses
To Grow a Hole the Size of Everything
Cosmic Lost and Found
Getting Karma's Goat
Gasconade
Tiny Chasm
Novel Cliche
Earthworms & Stars
Absolute Futility